This book belongs to

Date:_____

Vocabulary List Definitions and Sentences.

Word	
Definition	
Sentence	
Note	

Word	
Definition	
Sentence	
Note	

Word	
Definition	
Sentence	
Note	

Word	
Definition	
Sentence	
Note	

Word	
Definition	
Sentence	
Note	

Word	
Definition	
Sentence	
Note	

Date:_____

Vocabulary List Definitions and Sentences.

Word	
Definition	
Sentence	
Note	

Word	
Definition	
Sentence	
Note	

Word	
Definition	
Sentence	
Note	

Word	
Definition	
Sentence	
Note	

Word	
Definition	
Sentence	
Note	

Word	
Definition	
Sentence	
Note	

Date:_____

Vocabulary List Definitions and Sentences.

Word	
Definition	
Sentence	
Note	

Word	
Definition	
Sentence	
Note	

Word	
Definition	
Sentence	
Note	

Word	
Definition	
Sentence	
Note	

Word	
Definition	
Sentence	
Note	

Word	
Definition	
Sentence	
Note	

Date:_____

Vocabulary List Definitions and Sentences.

Word	
Definition	
Sentence	
Note	

Word	
Definition	
Sentence	
Note	

Word	
Definition	
Sentence	
Note	

Word	
Definition	
Sentence	
Note	

Word	
Definition	
Sentence	
Note	

Word	
Definition	
Sentence	
Note	

Date:_____

Vocabulary List Definitions and Sentences.

Word	
Definition	
Sentence	
Note	

Word	
Definition	
Sentence	
Note	

Word	
Definition	
Sentence	
Note	

Word	
Definition	
Sentence	
Note	

Word	
Definition	
Sentence	
Note	

Word	
Definition	
Sentence	
Note	

Date:_____

Vocabulary List Definitions and Sentences.

Word	
Definition	
Sentence	
Note	

Word	
Definition	
Sentence	
Note	

Word	
Definition	
Sentence	
Note	

Word	
Definition	
Sentence	
Note	

Word	
Definition	
Sentence	
Note	

Word	
Definition	
Sentence	
Note	

Date:_____

Vocabulary List Definitions and Sentences.

Word	
Definition	
Sentence	
Note	

Word	
Definition	
Sentence	
Note	

Word	
Definition	
Sentence	
Note	

Word	
Definition	
Sentence	
Note	

Word	
Definition	
Sentence	
Note	

Word	
Definition	
Sentence	
Note	

Date:_____

Vocabulary List Definitions and Sentences.

Word	
Definition	
Sentence	
Note	

Word	
Definition	
Sentence	
Note	

Word	
Definition	
Sentence	
Note	

Word	
Definition	
Sentence	
Note	

Word	
Definition	
Sentence	
Note	

Word	
Definition	
Sentence	
Note	

Date:_____

Vocabulary List Definitions and Sentences.

Word	
Definition	
Sentence	
Note	

Word	
Definition	
Sentence	
Note	

Word	
Definition	
Sentence	
Note	

Word	
Definition	
Sentence	
Note	

Word	
Definition	
Sentence	
Note	

Word	
Definition	
Sentence	
Note	

Date:_____

Vocabulary List Definitions and Sentences.

Word	
Definition	
Sentence	
Note	

Word	
Definition	
Sentence	
Note	

Word	
Definition	
Sentence	
Note	

Word	
Definition	
Sentence	
Note	

Word	
Definition	
Sentence	
Note	

Word	
Definition	
Sentence	
Note	

Date:_____

Vocabulary List Definitions and Sentences.

Word	
Definition	
Sentence	
Note	

Word	
Definition	
Sentence	
Note	

Word	
Definition	
Sentence	
Note	

Word	
Definition	
Sentence	
Note	

Word	
Definition	
Sentence	
Note	

Word	
Definition	
Sentence	
Note	

Date:_____

Vocabulary List Definitions and Sentences.

Word	
Definition	
Sentence	
Note	

Word	
Definition	
Sentence	
Note	

Word	
Definition	
Sentence	
Note	

Word	
Definition	
Sentence	
Note	

Word	
Definition	
Sentence	
Note	

Word	
Definition	
Sentence	
Note	

Date:_____

Vocabulary List Definitions and Sentences.

Word	
Definition	
Sentence	
Note	

Word	
Definition	
Sentence	
Note	

Word	
Definition	
Sentence	
Note	

Word	
Definition	
Sentence	
Note	

Word	
Definition	
Sentence	
Note	

Word	
Definition	
Sentence	
Note	

Date:_____

Vocabulary List Definitions and Sentences.

Word	
Definition	
Sentence	
Note	

Word	
Definition	
Sentence	
Note	

Word	
Definition	
Sentence	
Note	

Word	
Definition	
Sentence	
Note	

Word	
Definition	
Sentence	
Note	

Word	
Definition	
Sentence	
Note	

Date:_____

Vocabulary List Definitions and Sentences.

Word	
Definition	
Sentence	
Note	

Word	
Definition	
Sentence	
Note	

Word	
Definition	
Sentence	
Note	

Word	
Definition	
Sentence	
Note	

Word	
Definition	
Sentence	
Note	

Word	
Definition	
Sentence	
Note	

Date:_____

Vocabulary List Definitions and Sentences.

Word	
Definition	
Sentence	
Note	

Word	
Definition	
Sentence	
Note	

Word	
Definition	
Sentence	
Note	

Word	
Definition	
Sentence	
Note	

Word	
Definition	
Sentence	
Note	

Word	
Definition	
Sentence	
Note	

Date:_____

Vocabulary List Definitions and Sentences.

Word	
Definition	
Sentence	
Note	

Word	
Definition	
Sentence	
Note	

Word	
Definition	
Sentence	
Note	

Word	
Definition	
Sentence	
Note	

Word	
Definition	
Sentence	
Note	

Word	
Definition	
Sentence	
Note	

Date:_____

Vocabulary List Definitions and Sentences.

Word	
Definition	
Sentence	
Note	

Word	
Definition	
Sentence	
Note	

Word	
Definition	
Sentence	
Note	

Word	
Definition	
Sentence	
Note	

Word	
Definition	
Sentence	
Note	

Word	
Definition	
Sentence	
Note	

Date:_____

Vocabulary List Definitions and Sentences.

Word	
Definition	
Sentence	
Note	

Word	
Definition	
Sentence	
Note	

Word	
Definition	
Sentence	
Note	

Word	
Definition	
Sentence	
Note	

Word	
Definition	
Sentence	
Note	

Word	
Definition	
Sentence	
Note	

Date:_____

Vocabulary List Definitions and Sentences.

Word	
Definition	
Sentence	
Note	

Word	
Definition	
Sentence	
Note	

Word	
Definition	
Sentence	
Note	

Word	
Definition	
Sentence	
Note	

Word	
Definition	
Sentence	
Note	

Word	
Definition	
Sentence	
Note	

Date:_____

Vocabulary List Definitions and Sentences.

Word	
Definition	
Sentence	
Note	

Word	
Definition	
Sentence	
Note	

Word	
Definition	
Sentence	
Note	

Word	
Definition	
Sentence	
Note	

Word	
Definition	
Sentence	
Note	

Word	
Definition	
Sentence	
Note	

Date:_____

Vocabulary List Definitions and Sentences.

Word	
Definition	
Sentence	
Note	

Word	
Definition	
Sentence	
Note	

Word	
Definition	
Sentence	
Note	

Word	
Definition	
Sentence	
Note	

Word	
Definition	
Sentence	
Note	

Word	
Definition	
Sentence	
Note	

Date:_____

Vocabulary List Definitions and Sentences.

Word	
Definition	
Sentence	
Note	

Word	
Definition	
Sentence	
Note	

Word	
Definition	
Sentence	
Note	

Word	
Definition	
Sentence	
Note	

Word	
Definition	
Sentence	
Note	

Word	
Definition	
Sentence	
Note	

Date:_____

Vocabulary List Definitions and Sentences.

Word	
Definition	
Sentence	
Note	

Word	
Definition	
Sentence	
Note	

Word	
Definition	
Sentence	
Note	

Word	
Definition	
Sentence	
Note	

Word	
Definition	
Sentence	
Note	

Word	
Definition	
Sentence	
Note	

Date:_____

Vocabulary List Definitions and Sentences.

Word	
Definition	
Sentence	
Note	

Word	
Definition	
Sentence	
Note	

Word	
Definition	
Sentence	
Note	

Word	
Definition	
Sentence	
Note	

Word	
Definition	
Sentence	
Note	

Word	
Definition	
Sentence	
Note	

Date:_____

Vocabulary List Definitions and Sentences.

Word	
Definition	
Sentence	
Note	

Word	
Definition	
Sentence	
Note	

Word	
Definition	
Sentence	
Note	

Word	
Definition	
Sentence	
Note	

Word	
Definition	
Sentence	
Note	

Word	
Definition	
Sentence	
Note	

Date:_____

Vocabulary List Definitions and Sentences.

Word	
Definition	
Sentence	
Note	

Word	
Definition	
Sentence	
Note	

Word	
Definition	
Sentence	
Note	

Word	
Definition	
Sentence	
Note	

Word	
Definition	
Sentence	
Note	

Word	
Definition	
Sentence	
Note	

Date:_____

Vocabulary List Definitions and Sentences.

Word	
Definition	
Sentence	
Note	

Word	
Definition	
Sentence	
Note	

Word	
Definition	
Sentence	
Note	

Word	
Definition	
Sentence	
Note	

Word	
Definition	
Sentence	
Note	

Word	
Definition	
Sentence	
Note	

Date:_____

Vocabulary List Definitions and Sentences.

Word	
Definition	
Sentence	
Note	

Word	
Definition	
Sentence	
Note	

Word	
Definition	
Sentence	
Note	

Word	
Definition	
Sentence	
Note	

Word	
Definition	
Sentence	
Note	

Word	
Definition	
Sentence	
Note	

Date:_____

Vocabulary List Definitions and Sentences.

Word	
Definition	
Sentence	
Note	

Word	
Definition	
Sentence	
Note	

Word	
Definition	
Sentence	
Note	

Word	
Definition	
Sentence	
Note	

Word	
Definition	
Sentence	
Note	

Word	
Definition	
Sentence	
Note	

Date:_____

Vocabulary List Definitions and Sentences.

Word	
Definition	
Sentence	
Note	

Word	
Definition	
Sentence	
Note	

Word	
Definition	
Sentence	
Note	

Word	
Definition	
Sentence	
Note	

Word	
Definition	
Sentence	
Note	

Word	
Definition	
Sentence	
Note	

Date:_____

Vocabulary List Definitions and Sentences.

Word	
Definition	
Sentence	
Note	

Word	
Definition	
Sentence	
Note	

Word	
Definition	
Sentence	
Note	

Word	
Definition	
Sentence	
Note	

Word	
Definition	
Sentence	
Note	

Word	
Definition	
Sentence	
Note	

Date:_____

Vocabulary List Definitions and Sentences.

Word	
Definition	
Sentence	
Note	

Word	
Definition	
Sentence	
Note	

Word	
Definition	
Sentence	
Note	

Word	
Definition	
Sentence	
Note	

Word	
Definition	
Sentence	
Note	

Word	
Definition	
Sentence	
Note	

Date:_____

Vocabulary List Definitions and Sentences.

Word	
Definition	
Sentence	
Note	

Word	
Definition	
Sentence	
Note	

Word	
Definition	
Sentence	
Note	

Word	
Definition	
Sentence	
Note	

Word	
Definition	
Sentence	
Note	

Word	
Definition	
Sentence	
Note	

Date:_____

Vocabulary List Definitions and Sentences.

Word	
Definition	
Sentence	
Note	

Word	
Definition	
Sentence	
Note	

Word	
Definition	
Sentence	
Note	

Word	
Definition	
Sentence	
Note	

Word	
Definition	
Sentence	
Note	

Word	
Definition	
Sentence	
Note	

Date:_____

Vocabulary List Definitions and Sentences.

Word	
Definition	
Sentence	
Note	

Word	
Definition	
Sentence	
Note	

Word	
Definition	
Sentence	
Note	

Word	
Definition	
Sentence	
Note	

Word	
Definition	
Sentence	
Note	

Word	
Definition	
Sentence	
Note	

Date:_____

Vocabulary List Definitions and Sentences.

Word	
Definition	
Sentence	
Note	

Word	
Definition	
Sentence	
Note	

Word	
Definition	
Sentence	
Note	

Word	
Definition	
Sentence	
Note	

Word	
Definition	
Sentence	
Note	

Word	
Definition	
Sentence	
Note	

Date:_____

Vocabulary List Definitions and Sentences.

Word	
Definition	
Sentence	
Note	

Word	
Definition	
Sentence	
Note	

Word	
Definition	
Sentence	
Note	

Word	
Definition	
Sentence	
Note	

Word	
Definition	
Sentence	
Note	

Word	
Definition	
Sentence	
Note	

Date:_____

Vocabulary List Definitions and Sentences.

Word	
Definition	
Sentence	
Note	

Word	
Definition	
Sentence	
Note	

Word	
Definition	
Sentence	
Note	

Word	
Definition	
Sentence	
Note	

Word	
Definition	
Sentence	
Note	

Word	
Definition	
Sentence	
Note	

Date:_____

Vocabulary List Definitions and Sentences.

Word	
Definition	
Sentence	
Note	

Word	
Definition	
Sentence	
Note	

Word	
Definition	
Sentence	
Note	

Word	
Definition	
Sentence	
Note	

Word	
Definition	
Sentence	
Note	

Word	
Definition	
Sentence	
Note	

Date:_____

Vocabulary List Definitions and Sentences.

Word	
Definition	
Sentence	
Note	

Word	
Definition	
Sentence	
Note	

Word	
Definition	
Sentence	
Note	

Word	
Definition	
Sentence	
Note	

Word	
Definition	
Sentence	
Note	

Word	
Definition	
Sentence	
Note	

Date:_____

Vocabulary List Definitions and Sentences.

Word	
Definition	
Sentence	
Note	

Word	
Definition	
Sentence	
Note	

Word	
Definition	
Sentence	
Note	

Word	
Definition	
Sentence	
Note	

Word	
Definition	
Sentence	
Note	

Word	
Definition	
Sentence	
Note	

Date:_____

Vocabulary List Definitions and Sentences.

Word	
Definition	
Sentence	
Note	

Word	
Definition	
Sentence	
Note	

Word	
Definition	
Sentence	
Note	

Word	
Definition	
Sentence	
Note	

Word	
Definition	
Sentence	
Note	

Word	
Definition	
Sentence	
Note	

Date:_____

Vocabulary List Definitions and Sentences.

Word	
Definition	
Sentence	
Note	

Word	
Definition	
Sentence	
Note	

Word	
Definition	
Sentence	
Note	

Word	
Definition	
Sentence	
Note	

Word	
Definition	
Sentence	
Note	

Word	
Definition	
Sentence	
Note	

Date:_____

Vocabulary List Definitions and Sentences.

Word	
Definition	
Sentence	
Note	

Word	
Definition	
Sentence	
Note	

Word	
Definition	
Sentence	
Note	

Word	
Definition	
Sentence	
Note	

Word	
Definition	
Sentence	
Note	

Word	
Definition	
Sentence	
Note	

Date:_____

Vocabulary List Definitions and Sentences.

Word	
Definition	
Sentence	
Note	

Word	
Definition	
Sentence	
Note	

Word	
Definition	
Sentence	
Note	

Word	
Definition	
Sentence	
Note	

Word	
Definition	
Sentence	
Note	

Word	
Definition	
Sentence	
Note	

Date:_____

Vocabulary List Definitions and Sentences.

Word	
Definition	
Sentence	
Note	

Word	
Definition	
Sentence	
Note	

Word	
Definition	
Sentence	
Note	

Word	
Definition	
Sentence	
Note	

Word	
Definition	
Sentence	
Note	

Word	
Definition	
Sentence	
Note	

Date:_____

Vocabulary List Definitions and Sentences.

Word	
Definition	
Sentence	
Note	

Word	
Definition	
Sentence	
Note	

Word	
Definition	
Sentence	
Note	

Word	
Definition	
Sentence	
Note	

Word	
Definition	
Sentence	
Note	

Word	
Definition	
Sentence	
Note	

Date:_____

Vocabulary List Definitions and Sentences.

Word	
Definition	
Sentence	
Note	

Word	
Definition	
Sentence	
Note	

Word	
Definition	
Sentence	
Note	

Word	
Definition	
Sentence	
Note	

Word	
Definition	
Sentence	
Note	

Word	
Definition	
Sentence	
Note	

Date:_____

Vocabulary List Definitions and Sentences.

Word	
Definition	
Sentence	
Note	

Word	
Definition	
Sentence	
Note	

Word	
Definition	
Sentence	
Note	

Word	
Definition	
Sentence	
Note	

Word	
Definition	
Sentence	
Note	

Word	
Definition	
Sentence	
Note	

Date:_____

Vocabulary List Definitions and Sentences.

Word	
Definition	
Sentence	
Note	

Word	
Definition	
Sentence	
Note	

Word	
Definition	
Sentence	
Note	

Word	
Definition	
Sentence	
Note	

Word	
Definition	
Sentence	
Note	

Word	
Definition	
Sentence	
Note	

Date:_____

Vocabulary List Definitions and Sentences.

Word	
Definition	
Sentence	
Note	

Word	
Definition	
Sentence	
Note	

Word	
Definition	
Sentence	
Note	

Word	
Definition	
Sentence	
Note	

Word	
Definition	
Sentence	
Note	

Word	
Definition	
Sentence	
Note	

Date:_____

Vocabulary List Definitions and Sentences.

Word	
Definition	
Sentence	
Note	

Word	
Definition	
Sentence	
Note	

Word	
Definition	
Sentence	
Note	

Word	
Definition	
Sentence	
Note	

Word	
Definition	
Sentence	
Note	

Word	
Definition	
Sentence	
Note	

Date:_____

Vocabulary List Definitions and Sentences.

Word	
Definition	
Sentence	
Note	

Word	
Definition	
Sentence	
Note	

Word	
Definition	
Sentence	
Note	

Word	
Definition	
Sentence	
Note	

Word	
Definition	
Sentence	
Note	

Word	
Definition	
Sentence	
Note	

Date:_____

Vocabulary List Definitions and Sentences.

Word	
Definition	
Sentence	
Note	

Word	
Definition	
Sentence	
Note	

Word	
Definition	
Sentence	
Note	

Word	
Definition	
Sentence	
Note	

Word	
Definition	
Sentence	
Note	

Word	
Definition	
Sentence	
Note	

Date:_____

Vocabulary List Definitions and Sentences.

Word	
Definition	
Sentence	
Note	

Word	
Definition	
Sentence	
Note	

Word	
Definition	
Sentence	
Note	

Word	
Definition	
Sentence	
Note	

Word	
Definition	
Sentence	
Note	

Word	
Definition	
Sentence	
Note	

Date:_____

Vocabulary List Definitions and Sentences.

Word	
Definition	
Sentence	
Note	

Word	
Definition	
Sentence	
Note	

Word	
Definition	
Sentence	
Note	

Word	
Definition	
Sentence	
Note	

Word	
Definition	
Sentence	
Note	

Word	
Definition	
Sentence	
Note	

Date:_____

Vocabulary List Definitions and Sentences.

Word	
Definition	
Sentence	
Note	

Word	
Definition	
Sentence	
Note	

Word	
Definition	
Sentence	
Note	

Word	
Definition	
Sentence	
Note	

Word	
Definition	
Sentence	
Note	

Word	
Definition	
Sentence	
Note	

Date:_____

Vocabulary List Definitions and Sentences.

Word	
Definition	
Sentence	
Note	

Word	
Definition	
Sentence	
Note	

Word	
Definition	
Sentence	
Note	

Word	
Definition	
Sentence	
Note	

Word	
Definition	
Sentence	
Note	

Word	
Definition	
Sentence	
Note	

Date:_____

Vocabulary List Definitions and Sentences.

Word	
Definition	
Sentence	
Note	

Word	
Definition	
Sentence	
Note	

Word	
Definition	
Sentence	
Note	

Word	
Definition	
Sentence	
Note	

Word	
Definition	
Sentence	
Note	

Word	
Definition	
Sentence	
Note	

Date:_____

Vocabulary List Definitions and Sentences.

Word	
Definition	
Sentence	
Note	

Word	
Definition	
Sentence	
Note	

Word	
Definition	
Sentence	
Note	

Word	
Definition	
Sentence	
Note	

Word	
Definition	
Sentence	
Note	

Word	
Definition	
Sentence	
Note	

Date:_____

Vocabulary List Definitions and Sentences.

Word	
Definition	
Sentence	
Note	

Word	
Definition	
Sentence	
Note	

Word	
Definition	
Sentence	
Note	

Word	
Definition	
Sentence	
Note	

Word	
Definition	
Sentence	
Note	

Word	
Definition	
Sentence	
Note	

Date:_____

Vocabulary List Definitions and Sentences.

Word	
Definition	
Sentence	
Note	

Word	
Definition	
Sentence	
Note	

Word	
Definition	
Sentence	
Note	

Word	
Definition	
Sentence	
Note	

Word	
Definition	
Sentence	
Note	

Word	
Definition	
Sentence	
Note	

Date:_____

Vocabulary List Definitions and Sentences.

Word	
Definition	
Sentence	
Note	

Word	
Definition	
Sentence	
Note	

Word	
Definition	
Sentence	
Note	

Word	
Definition	
Sentence	
Note	

Word	
Definition	
Sentence	
Note	

Word	
Definition	
Sentence	
Note	

Date:_____

Vocabulary List Definitions and Sentences.

Word	
Definition	
Sentence	
Note	

Word	
Definition	
Sentence	
Note	

Word	
Definition	
Sentence	
Note	

Word	
Definition	
Sentence	
Note	

Word	
Definition	
Sentence	
Note	

Word	
Definition	
Sentence	
Note	

Date:_____

Vocabulary List Definitions and Sentences.

Word	
Definition	
Sentence	
Note	

Word	
Definition	
Sentence	
Note	

Word	
Definition	
Sentence	
Note	

Word	
Definition	
Sentence	
Note	

Word	
Definition	
Sentence	
Note	

Word	
Definition	
Sentence	
Note	

Date:_____

Vocabulary List Definitions and Sentences.

Word	
Definition	
Sentence	
Note	

Word	
Definition	
Sentence	
Note	

Word	
Definition	
Sentence	
Note	

Word	
Definition	
Sentence	
Note	

Word	
Definition	
Sentence	
Note	

Word	
Definition	
Sentence	
Note	

Date:_____

Vocabulary List Definitions and Sentences.

Word	
Definition	
Sentence	
Note	

Word	
Definition	
Sentence	
Note	

Word	
Definition	
Sentence	
Note	

Word	
Definition	
Sentence	
Note	

Word	
Definition	
Sentence	
Note	

Word	
Definition	
Sentence	
Note	

Date:_____

Vocabulary List Definitions and Sentences.

Word	
Definition	
Sentence	
Note	

Word	
Definition	
Sentence	
Note	

Word	
Definition	
Sentence	
Note	

Word	
Definition	
Sentence	
Note	

Word	
Definition	
Sentence	
Note	

Word	
Definition	
Sentence	
Note	

Date:_____

Vocabulary List Definitions and Sentences.

Word	
Definition	
Sentence	
Note	

Word	
Definition	
Sentence	
Note	

Word	
Definition	
Sentence	
Note	

Word	
Definition	
Sentence	
Note	

Word	
Definition	
Sentence	
Note	

Word	
Definition	
Sentence	
Note	

Date:_____

Vocabulary List Definitions and Sentences.

Word	
Definition	
Sentence	
Note	

Word	
Definition	
Sentence	
Note	

Word	
Definition	
Sentence	
Note	

Word	
Definition	
Sentence	
Note	

Word	
Definition	
Sentence	
Note	

Word	
Definition	
Sentence	
Note	

Date:_____

Vocabulary List Definitions and Sentences.

Word	
Definition	
Sentence	
Note	

Word	
Definition	
Sentence	
Note	

Word	
Definition	
Sentence	
Note	

Word	
Definition	
Sentence	
Note	

Word	
Definition	
Sentence	
Note	

Word	
Definition	
Sentence	
Note	

Date:_____

Vocabulary List Definitions and Sentences.

Word	
Definition	
Sentence	
Note	

Word	
Definition	
Sentence	
Note	

Word	
Definition	
Sentence	
Note	

Word	
Definition	
Sentence	
Note	

Word	
Definition	
Sentence	
Note	

Word	
Definition	
Sentence	
Note	

Date:_____

Vocabulary List Definitions and Sentences.

Word	
Definition	
Sentence	
Note	

Word	
Definition	
Sentence	
Note	

Word	
Definition	
Sentence	
Note	

Word	
Definition	
Sentence	
Note	

Word	
Definition	
Sentence	
Note	

Word	
Definition	
Sentence	
Note	

Date:_____

Vocabulary List Definitions and Sentences.

Word	
Definition	
Sentence	
Note	

Word	
Definition	
Sentence	
Note	

Word	
Definition	
Sentence	
Note	

Word	
Definition	
Sentence	
Note	

Word	
Definition	
Sentence	
Note	

Word	
Definition	
Sentence	
Note	

Date:_____

Vocabulary List Definitions and Sentences.

Word	
Definition	
Sentence	
Note	

Word	
Definition	
Sentence	
Note	

Word	
Definition	
Sentence	
Note	

Word	
Definition	
Sentence	
Note	

Word	
Definition	
Sentence	
Note	

Word	
Definition	
Sentence	
Note	

Date:_____

Vocabulary List Definitions and Sentences.

Word	
Definition	
Sentence	
Note	

Word	
Definition	
Sentence	
Note	

Word	
Definition	
Sentence	
Note	

Word	
Definition	
Sentence	
Note	

Word	
Definition	
Sentence	
Note	

Word	
Definition	
Sentence	
Note	

Date:_____

Vocabulary List Definitions and Sentences.

Word	
Definition	
Sentence	
Note	

Word	
Definition	
Sentence	
Note	

Word	
Definition	
Sentence	
Note	

Word	
Definition	
Sentence	
Note	

Word	
Definition	
Sentence	
Note	

Word	
Definition	
Sentence	
Note	

Date:_____

Vocabulary List Definitions and Sentences.

Word	
Definition	
Sentence	
Note	

Word	
Definition	
Sentence	
Note	

Word	
Definition	
Sentence	
Note	

Word	
Definition	
Sentence	
Note	

Word	
Definition	
Sentence	
Note	

Word	
Definition	
Sentence	
Note	

Date:_____

Vocabulary List Definitions and Sentences.

Word	
Definition	
Sentence	
Note	

Word	
Definition	
Sentence	
Note	

Word	
Definition	
Sentence	
Note	

Word	
Definition	
Sentence	
Note	

Word	
Definition	
Sentence	
Note	

Word	
Definition	
Sentence	
Note	

Date:_____

Vocabulary List Definitions and Sentences.

Word	
Definition	
Sentence	
Note	

Word	
Definition	
Sentence	
Note	

Word	
Definition	
Sentence	
Note	

Word	
Definition	
Sentence	
Note	

Word	
Definition	
Sentence	
Note	

Word	
Definition	
Sentence	
Note	

Date:_____

Vocabulary List Definitions and Sentences.

Word	
Definition	
Sentence	
Note	

Word	
Definition	
Sentence	
Note	

Word	
Definition	
Sentence	
Note	

Word	
Definition	
Sentence	
Note	

Word	
Definition	
Sentence	
Note	

Word	
Definition	
Sentence	
Note	

Date:_____

Vocabulary List Definitions and Sentences.

Word	
Definition	
Sentence	
Note	

Word	
Definition	
Sentence	
Note	

Word	
Definition	
Sentence	
Note	

Word	
Definition	
Sentence	
Note	

Word	
Definition	
Sentence	
Note	

Word	
Definition	
Sentence	
Note	

Date:_____

Vocabulary List Definitions and Sentences.

Word	
Definition	
Sentence	
Note	

Word	
Definition	
Sentence	
Note	

Word	
Definition	
Sentence	
Note	

Word	
Definition	
Sentence	
Note	

Word	
Definition	
Sentence	
Note	

Word	
Definition	
Sentence	
Note	

Date:_____

Vocabulary List Definitions and Sentences.

Word	
Definition	
Sentence	
Note	

Word	
Definition	
Sentence	
Note	

Word	
Definition	
Sentence	
Note	

Word	
Definition	
Sentence	
Note	

Word	
Definition	
Sentence	
Note	

Word	
Definition	
Sentence	
Note	

Date:_____

Vocabulary List Definitions and Sentences.

Word	
Definition	
Sentence	
Note	

Word	
Definition	
Sentence	
Note	

Word	
Definition	
Sentence	
Note	

Word	
Definition	
Sentence	
Note	

Word	
Definition	
Sentence	
Note	

Word	
Definition	
Sentence	
Note	

Date:_____

Vocabulary List Definitions and Sentences.

Word	
Definition	
Sentence	
Note	

Word	
Definition	
Sentence	
Note	

Word	
Definition	
Sentence	
Note	

Word	
Definition	
Sentence	
Note	

Word	
Definition	
Sentence	
Note	

Word	
Definition	
Sentence	
Note	

Date:_____

Vocabulary List Definitions and Sentences.

Word	
Definition	
Sentence	
Note	

Word	
Definition	
Sentence	
Note	

Word	
Definition	
Sentence	
Note	

Word	
Definition	
Sentence	
Note	

Word	
Definition	
Sentence	
Note	

Word	
Definition	
Sentence	
Note	

Date:_____

Vocabulary List Definitions and Sentences.

Word	
Definition	
Sentence	
Note	

Word	
Definition	
Sentence	
Note	

Word	
Definition	
Sentence	
Note	

Word	
Definition	
Sentence	
Note	

Word	
Definition	
Sentence	
Note	

Word	
Definition	
Sentence	
Note	

Date:_____

Vocabulary List Definitions and Sentences.

Word	
Definition	
Sentence	
Note	

Word	
Definition	
Sentence	
Note	

Word	
Definition	
Sentence	
Note	

Word	
Definition	
Sentence	
Note	

Word	
Definition	
Sentence	
Note	

Word	
Definition	
Sentence	
Note	

Date:_____

Vocabulary List Definitions and Sentences.

Word	
Definition	
Sentence	
Note	

Word	
Definition	
Sentence	
Note	

Word	
Definition	
Sentence	
Note	

Word	
Definition	
Sentence	
Note	

Word	
Definition	
Sentence	
Note	

Word	
Definition	
Sentence	
Note	

Date:_____

Vocabulary List Definitions and Sentences.

Word	
Definition	
Sentence	
Note	

Word	
Definition	
Sentence	
Note	

Word	
Definition	
Sentence	
Note	

Word	
Definition	
Sentence	
Note	

Word	
Definition	
Sentence	
Note	

Word	
Definition	
Sentence	
Note	

Date:_____

Vocabulary List Definitions and Sentences.

Word	
Definition	
Sentence	
Note	

Word	
Definition	
Sentence	
Note	

Word	
Definition	
Sentence	
Note	

Word	
Definition	
Sentence	
Note	

Word	
Definition	
Sentence	
Note	

Word	
Definition	
Sentence	
Note	

Date:_____

Vocabulary List Definitions and Sentences.

Word	
Definition	
Sentence	
Note	

Word	
Definition	
Sentence	
Note	

Word	
Definition	
Sentence	
Note	

Word	
Definition	
Sentence	
Note	

Word	
Definition	
Sentence	
Note	

Word	
Definition	
Sentence	
Note	

Date:_____

Vocabulary List Definitions and Sentences.

Word	
Definition	
Sentence	
Note	

Word	
Definition	
Sentence	
Note	

Word	
Definition	
Sentence	
Note	

Word	
Definition	
Sentence	
Note	

Word	
Definition	
Sentence	
Note	

Word	
Definition	
Sentence	
Note	

Date:_____

Vocabulary List Definitions and Sentences.

Word	
Definition	
Sentence	
Note	

Word	
Definition	
Sentence	
Note	

Word	
Definition	
Sentence	
Note	

Word	
Definition	
Sentence	
Note	

Word	
Definition	
Sentence	
Note	

Word	
Definition	
Sentence	
Note	

Date:_____

Vocabulary List Definitions and Sentences.

Word	
Definition	
Sentence	
Note	

Word	
Definition	
Sentence	
Note	

Word	
Definition	
Sentence	
Note	

Word	
Definition	
Sentence	
Note	

Word	
Definition	
Sentence	
Note	

Word	
Definition	
Sentence	
Note	

Date:_____

Vocabulary List Definitions and Sentences.

Word	
Definition	
Sentence	
Note	

Word	
Definition	
Sentence	
Note	

Word	
Definition	
Sentence	
Note	

Word	
Definition	
Sentence	
Note	

Word	
Definition	
Sentence	
Note	

Word	
Definition	
Sentence	
Note	

Printed in Great Britain
by Amazon